How Do Haiti Presidential Term Limits

Impact the Long Term Stability of the Country?

Rousseau, Bobb Q

Presidential Term Limits

Copyright © 2014 by Rousseau, Bobb Q

To the members of the civil society

To Law, Political Science, and Administrative Law students

To the Haitian Government

Preface

Generally, it is almost impossible to start a debate about Haiti without mentioning the past and present architecture of its politic, functioning as a ritual for social, cultural, and industrial misadventure leading to the country's degrading economic conditions. Today, we will not be talking about government corruption, insecurity, and foreign assistance dependence; but we will be talking about a possible root of such instability.

While everyone is blaming our officials (both elected and appointed) for their political greed, their lack of interest for the nation welfare, and their inattentiveness to the people' needs; after extensive researches, consultation of scholarly references, conversation with the people, observation of over a generation of political history, and after conducting a slew of interviews through which the people of Haiti have spoken, I found myself wondering whether the framers of the Constitution of Haiti of 1987 had not shaped the conditions or provided the legal and historical framework to become corrupted as well as to reward bad behaviors.

I am neither justifying nor am I defending crooked politicians nor I am not forgiving circuitous governments for extorting and denying Haitians the opportunities to fulfill economic freedom and political emancipation. I am advancing that the problem can only be fixed when approached intelligently and when the causes are known.

There are several articles in the Constitution that afford that bait on which our officials are hooked and henceforth becoming addicted to immorality and a "don't care attitude" toward the country. Article 12.1 that sweeps away the Haitian diaspora from their civil rights is one of the causes of Haitian intellectual poverty for it encourages brain drain; a phenomenon where the intelligentsia migrates to other countries, creating an opportunistic void for individuals to convert themselves into politicians with no political sense to develop social programs and to negotiate with the International Community urging them to apply relevant aid to relevant sectors of the country.

We cannot not talk about Article 134.4 prescribing term limits for Presidents as a factor that also tramples individual's freedom and civil liberties; no more than two terms of five years each and these two terms cannot be consecutive. Confusing, is not it? My mission was to find out the rationale behind such a constitutional restriction and whether such a constitutional restriction made an accent of political sense. So, I conducted this research and I want to share with you the results of my findings.

"Presidential Term Limits: Their Impacts on the Long Term Stability of Haiti" is a must read book. The author starts his study with a tranche of the pride Haitian history and trickles it down to our current history. Hopefully, you, after reading this, will take the appropriate actions to hold government officials responsible for the sad path toward political catastrophe and social upheaval.

Bobb Q

Foreword

All elected functions in Haiti may be reelected an unlimited number of times except that of the President. Furthermore, all of these elected officials can serve several terms consecutively whereas Presidents cannot whom, according to article 134.3 of the current Constitution; can only serve two terms with a five-year gap between their two terms.

Why such a cap on only Presidents? It is because House Representatives, Senators, Mayors, CASECs, and ASECS are closer to the people or it is because the framers of the Constitution of 1987 wanted to prevent another dictatorship? It is because the Constitution wants to ensure that more individuals run and become Presidents or is it because that same Constitution wants to promote successful presidential transitions? The golden and million-dollar question is "Is such a constitutional restriction in fashion with the will of the people or should not the people have the right to vote for whomever they want as many times they want? Lastly, how does such a probation period advance necessary democracy in Haiti or is not such a restraint at the root of Haiti's political, social, cultural, economic, developmental, and industrial instability?

Bobb answers all these questions in this book. Better yet, he asks you these questions and you provide him with the answers, which he scientifically collects, analyzes, and compiles in order to further a new political approach to people interested in the sustainable progress of Haiti.

First, the cover displays an ancient look, ancient not because the chapters retell a period of Haitian history, but because they convey a fashionable and classic appeal. He starts the book with a tranche of history where he refreshed our memory with the refusal of Nissage Saget to serve as President as well as the popular action of the nation pressuring Congress to nominate Sylvain Salnave as their President. He later tells us that the notions of presidential term limits and popular elections are fairly new in Haitian politics. In fact, the first time they make standings in Haiti was with the vote of the Constitution of 1987.

Bobb gives us a meticulous background of such a phenomenon backed up by a scholarly literature review. He walks us through the study, telling us step by step what he intends to do and at times, in case we get distracted or lost, he reminds us what the study describes and what the conclusion might be. The visual aids such as charts and figures are explained with numbers and words that empower us to understand and predict the outcomes. When we reach the end of the book, we muster the feeling that we just got schooled in our own history, making us smarter than when we started.

This is the second edition of the book. It contains more background information, more data collection and more data analysis, and it is written more intelligently. This shows the researcher intellectual growth and his commitment toward revising and reediting his works because no work can be claimed to be perfect or set in stones. What makes the second edition more relevant is that Bobb applies deeper reasoning and tougher critical thinking; he had conducted more extensive researches, and had interviewed a wider sample of Haitians in order to formulate his unbiased and ethical judgment on the real impacts of Haiti's Presidential term limits on the country's long term stability.

I encourage you to purchase and read this book. After you read it, share it with your friends, your family, or on your Facebook page, but make sure you keep a copy to yourself. I guarantee you that you will refer to its contents each time your will try to understand why civil wars, political unrests, elections rigging and governmental frauds have been plaguing the country since 1987.

Dr. Laura Kolberg-White

Table of Contents

Abstract.. 1

A Tranche of Haitian History.. 3

Background 7

Research Questions and Hypotheses 11

Literature Review... 23

Who Can Be President of Haiti?.. 27

History of Haiti's Presidential Term Limits 29

Methodology 33

Results 39

Summary 43

Conclusion.. 45

References 47

Abstract

Civil wars, demonstrations, elections rigging, governmental frauds, wastes, abuses, unrests, leadership corruption, drug trafficking, insecurity, etc., meshed with a succession of governments, be they are democratic or dictatorial, have been the highlights of Haitian's politics since the day of its Independence in 1804. In spite of the pouring of foreign assistance, the country's Growth Development Product (GPD) remains below standard of the United Nations (UN) requirements. Thus, Haiti has been considered as the poorest country of the Western hemisphere. And yet, the people continue to vote on demands because they hope for changes and opportunities. Unfortunately, Presidents come and go; the majority of them without even achieving a meager of what they promise throughout their campaigns. Those who seemingly are willing to bring comprehensive changes into government institutions and into the people' lives do not last long enough to implement their social programs to their fullest. This is due mainly to the principle of power alternations, known as presidential term limits, imposed by Article 134.3 of the Constitution of the country. The study assesses whether relationships exist between Haiti's Presidential terms limit and the long-term stability of the country. It furthermore assess whether presidential term limit, especially the five-year probation, restraints the capacity of leaders nearing their term to fully engage in foreign negotiations and domestic policies as well as whether it denies the people the democratic right to vote for as many times they want for the candidate of their choice. Analyzing interview-data collected from two segments of the general population, it recommends and generates the application of a new theory and concludes by explaining the five-year probation promotes unnecessary democracy in Haiti.

Keywords: power alternations, democratic polity, political survival, diversity in governance.

A Tranche of Haitian History

The notions of presidential term limits and popular elections do not have long-standing roots in Haitian politics. In fact, it was the responsibility of the Senate, meeting in Constituent Assembly to nominate individuals to serve as Presidents for as long as they wished. The first time the nation expressed their freedom on choosing their President was on May 2, 1867 when they organized themselves to acclaim Sylvain Salnave, after he led the overthrow of Fabre Geffrard as their next President soon after Nissage Saget refused the Senate nomination. The Senate had no other obligation to select Salnave who had led the country from 14 June to 13 December 1869 although he was supposed to serve four years.

The previous Emperors and Presidents were not restricted to specific limits. As a matter of fact, most of them were overthrown while a few of them died in powers. The notion of term limits officially appeared in Haitian politics with the enactment of the Constitution of 1987 in its article 134.3 regulating the amount of time a person could serve as President. The Constitution established two-term limits worth five years each with a five-year probation period, serving as a vital check against any one person accumulating too much power.

The way it works is that Presidents are elected for five years. Before reaching the end of their terms, they are required to organize elections through which they relinquish powers to new Presidents. They are furthermore re-eligible to run for presidencies after five years. Should

Rousseau, Bobb Q

they win, they will be serving another five years. In simpler terms, Presidents serve for 10 years, but not consecutively; there is a five year break between the two terms.

It was in virtue of such a probation period that Jean-Bertrand Aristide and René Préval were elected Presidents of Haiti twice or the party Lavalas had remained in powers for 20 years. It is in virtue of such probation that Michel Martelly already picked his Prime Minister, Laurent Lamothe, to be his successor. It might be in virtue of such probation that Martelly's political party might remain in powers for at least 20 years.

Article 134.1 is the straightest to the point and the most clear-cut article of the Constitution. It does only have one legislative interpretation; no two consecutive terms and under no circumstance, a third term is permitted. Haitian lawmakers intended to create a two-term tradition in order to promote power alternations, democratic polity, and successful transitions. However, historical data had shown that the intentions of such an article has not being met and rather functioning as a political necessity; it generates instability where sitting Presidents are compelled to deal with ongoing unrests and undue protestations tailored by the opposing camp requesting their departure or changes in governments.

Haitian lawmakers and members of the civil society do not seem to see any issue with presidential term limits, especially the five-year gap between the constitutional prescribed two-terms. René Préval was the first and so far the only Haitian official to have made it known to the public that the probation period was at the root of Haiti's long term political instability. Various people tend to agree with Préval's assess-

4

ment but it has yet to catch up with Congress who should be taking necessary steps to address and possibly enact measures preventing the emergence of political parties backed up with long and bogus tenures. In addition to be at the roots of the country's political instability, term limits disqualify first termed President who may be advancing the nation welfare from running for another period, which impedes continuity in public administration.

This study answers several questions:

1. Did Haitian lawmakers meet their intent from preventing Presidents and their political party from building their own empire?

2. Are presidential term limits, especially the probation period a necessity, bad or good democracy for Haiti?

3. What are the impacts (if any) of presidential term on the country's long term stability?

4. Does the probation period remove the power to reelect from voters?

5. Who should have the authority to decide whether Presidents deserve two consecutive, a third, or to serve infinitively?

The people of Haiti provide answers to these questions. The researcher selects a sample representing the general population to whom he administered a questionnaire survey. Answers were collected and analyzed and it was found that the time has come to end the presidential probation period, because continuing the restrictions on how long one can serve in highest office is bad democracy for the country. It gives first time-sitting presidents strong ammunitions to govern in campaign modes so they can endorse or select their replacement and the wheel keeps on rolling where the same political party might be in powers for at least 20 years. It also allows second-term presidents to enact midnight public policies in order to attract foreign investments; henceforward they are likely to implement bogus social programs that poorly justify funds collected.

Background

Term limits are laid down in Articles 63, 68, 92, 78 and 134 of the Constitution of Haiti of 1987 in order to set a maximum number of years for leadership tenures. It is four years for members of the Administrative Councils of the Communal Sections (CASECs) and that of Assemblies of the Communal Sections (ASECs). It is also four years for Mayors and Deputies, six years for Senators, and five years for Presidents. All these positions, except that of the President may be reelected an unlimited number of times. Only in Haiti, the concept of presidential term limits is so extreme and so two folded. In fact, article 134.3 of the Constitution states that "No person shall be elected as President of Haiti more than twice and no person who holds such offices shall serve two five-year consecutive terms." Henceforth, there is a five-year probation period Presidents must undergo before they re-become eligible to run for a second term.

Besides its high rate of poverty and its continuous threads of violence, Haiti is known as a country where elections are always rigged and where Presidents are always corrupted. Campaign speeches are never transformed into viable actions and the people suffer from poor leaderships. Presidential elections are organized every five years or so in Haiti, which is to contend that the right to vote is guaranteed and protected but whether Presidents implement commonsense measures to provide economic freedom to their voters is to be desired. They run their campaigns on energizing the people to vote for them while promising them hopes and opportunities to pursue the human dream. However, after winning these elections, their campaign speeches are put on the back burner. The reason may be that they do not have the resources necessary to develop comprehensive social programs such as education, healthcare, jobs, etc. Consequently, they are forced to rely on foreign assistance to provide for the people. It is assumed that Presidents cannot perform well because their plans are often overcome by events where once they begin to acquire presidential maturity; it is already time for elections, which they are not eligible to participate (Art. 134.3 of the Constitution of Haiti of 1987) and more than likely their plans will not be continued by their successors.

This research comes to light after a series of observations ranging since 1990 where Presidents are elected for five years, leave their seat to go in campaign modes for five years and return to their original seat for five more years. We believe that such "come, go and return" strategy hinders Presidents from finishing projects that were introduced by their regime, which in turn affect the economy in the sense that policies introduced by outgoing Presidents cease to be implemented by incoming presidents and when they return, they are likely to not return to their old agenda or to not continue that of their predecessors and thus they will enact new policies. It also impacts foreign relations where the International Community would act reluctant to negotiate with presidents nearing their final stretch.

This research is necessary for it will allow the researcher to interview random Haitians in order to collect their subjective thoughts on the matter of Haiti's Presidential term limits. Using computer software package such as Nvivo, data collected will be objectively analyzed and coded to find recurring themes or short phrases that will prove or disprove whether term limit is at the root of the country's long term stability, whether it hinders the continuity of domestic policies, whether it hampers foreign relations or whether the people should have a say on how long they want to be governed by one President. Here, the term "stability" refers to the fluctuations of Haitian politics and the deplorable economic of the Haitian, which are both critical to their ability to draw domestic and foreign investments toward Haiti required for a self-sustainable country (Voices of America, 2012) and Hanson (2006).

Problem Statement

Term limits normally mean a maximum of two terms, each of which does not exceed five years and both terms separated by a five-year probation period (Constitution of Haiti, 1987, Art. 134.3). Covensky (2007) refers to this constitutional restriction, as "democratic polity" as it guarantees power alternations and provides the assurance that another party will win the next elections. The five-year period Presidents must wait before becoming eligible to run for a second term and the restriction to run for a third term have various impacts on foreign relations and the continuity of domestic policies. New Presidents come every five years along with them new policies and second termed presidents are compelled to either follow up with their original policies or enact new ones, which affects the country's long term stability.

Purpose of the Study

Applying the grounded theory and the case study qualitative approaches through which the researcher will conduct one structured and one unstructured interviews after the observation of 25 years of political history (Creswell, 2013), this paper will explore three principal impacts of Haiti's presidential term limits, will develop a commonsense rationale to show the impacts of phenomenon in question on Haiti's long term stability, to constructively propose the removal of the probation period, and recommend the application of the referendum theory, which will allow the people to decide and whether the decision whether a president deserves two consecutive, a third, a fourth, or more terms, be left to them.

Research Questions and Hypotheses

I t is assumed that the presidential term limits have huge impacts on foreign relations, domestic policies, and democracy. To effectively measure these impacts (if any), it is important to formulate overreaching or open-ended research questions, which will facilitate the exploration of the topic in question. It is decided that such an investigation will require one central question. It is furthermore decided that this research will not have sub questions, but instead, it will have three hypotheses, which will seek to establish relationships between term limits, foreign policies, domestic policies, and democracy.

Central Question

How does Haiti's presidential term limit, especially the five-year probation, affect political and economic stabilities in Haiti?

According to Griner (2009) "presidential term limits is the main cause of public distrust in democratic institutions. It is a significant obstacle to economic development transpiring corruption." In 1987, the Haitian people voted a new Constitution, which prescribed the form of a new government in order to divorce with the dictatorship environment of the Duvaliers that lasted 30 years. From 1986 to 1990, several attempts of organizing elections failed due a reluctant acceptance of the new democratic setup. With the help of the International Community, in 1990, the country held its first free and fair elections in Haiti where in 1991, a former Catholic priest Jean-Bertrand Aristide was elected as the president. Eight months later, he was overthrown by the Haitian military and he entered into a forced exile in the United States of America. He returned to power three years later where he completed the remaining eight months of his initial term. Thereafter, he organized elections to cede the place to his best friend René Préval in 1996 while, although he was not the President, he remained the most influential political leader in Haiti. This was the very first time in over almost 50 years that the nation had witnessed a democratic and successful transfer of powers between two presidents (Mark, 2004). Five years later, Préval organized elections where he ceded powers to Aristide, who once again, following a flood of continued accusations of corruptions and repeated humans rights violations, was removed from his position to be sent into exile in 1994 to South Africa.

Thereafter, a succession of interim governments, which organized another yet free and fair election, succeeded him and Préval returned to the presidential seat. In 2010, not allowed to run for a third term and pressured by Mr. Barrack Obama and Mr. Bill Clinton, he organized elections from which he passed the torch to Mr. Michel Martelly. Although Aristide and Préval were members of the same political movement; they exhibited differently leadership styles and each time they returned, they reinvented their leadership styles mostly for the worst. The country did learn to adjust and adapt to both styles, which did not offer any kind of political stability nor did they promote necessary democracy or social justice.

Hypotheses

Creswell (2013) suggested that hypotheses are the recommended methods for proving or   disproving research theories. In this section, hypotheses will be developed to demonstrate the impacts of presidential term limits on foreign relations and public policies and thereafter on social justice.

Hypothesis 1: The presidential term limit decreases the effectiveness of Presidents to pursue and strengthen foreign relations?

The President of the Republic of Haiti is constitutionally authorized to set foreign policies for the nation. As such, he negotiates and signs all international treaties, conventions, and agreements. He makes decisions establishing relationships between his country and other nations. He negotiates with the International Community on monetary and humanitarian aids for the country. He represents the people in international summits and pleads their cases before appropriate entities (Art. 139.1). Very often, if it is not always, his decisions, whether bad or good, last beyond his term in offices. Holding a lame duck status or approaching the end of their tenure, the International Community behaves reluctant to negotiate with them because they are losing Congress and the people' support.

The Préval administration had launched policies that attracted the United Nations and the rest of the International Community who were convinced that finally Haiti was making a go to claim and obtain a seat at the concert of democratic nations. Many foreign policies were enacted and interests in the impoverished nation reached its peaks so much that the Poverty Reduction Strategy succeeded in relieving the debts of the country according to IMF requirements. Economic assistance came from world donors and investors and with relentless aids and relevant international supports, between 2004 and 2009, Upchurch and Mathers

(2009) reported that Haiti was able to reach the standard growth mark of IMF.

However, less than six months near his final term and although the country was recovering from a terrible earthquake that same year, the United States and the International Community made it clear that they no longer wanted to deal with René Préval when it came to providing humanitarian assistance to the people. They dealt directly with the Prime Minister, Mr. Jean-Max Bellerive and in most cases with various Non-Governmental Organizations (NGOs) dispersed throughout the country. In fact, Mr. Obama declared on US national television that the only entity authorized to collect humanitarian funds for Haiti was the American Red Cross (Forman, Lang, and Chandler, 2011).

Because of that terrible earthquake that destroyed 90% of the country infrastructures, killed over 250.000 people and left 1.3 million people homeless (Goldberg, 2013), the country was not ready for elections. The people of Haiti knew that, the politicians knew that, but Barrack Obama and Bill Clinton pushed so hard for the respect of article 134.2 of the constitution, which suggests that Presidential elections be held the last Sunday of November in the fifth year of the President's term. Préval had no choice to organize the elections because America wanted a full termed President with whom to negotiate future aids to Haiti. The UN, through Mr. Edmond Mullet, at that time Assistant Secretary-General for Peacekeeping Operations, was instrumental in scheduling and publishing elections dates and updates. Such an action made Préval insignificant and while out of the country for a visit to the Dominican Republic, the embassies of France, Canada, and The United States

14

invaded the premises of the Provisional Electoral Council [manu military] where they ordered its members to publish new results, which put an end to speculations of elections riggings and frauds that suggested Ms. Mirlande Manigat, member of the Rally of Progressive National Democrats (RDNP) and Mr. Jude Celestin, unknown to the International Community, but a protégé of René Préval were going on a run off. The latter name was removed and these embassies added the name of Michel Martelly [who later won the 2011 elections at 67% of the popular votes] to face off Madame Mirlande Manigat (Archobold, 2011).

Although half-way of his second term, he publically showed his lack of interests for the country by encouraging the nation to "swim to get out of the country mess," Préval was still relying on his positions to negotiate with foreign nations about strategic planning to receive and distribute critical aids to the victims of the earthquake of 12 January 2010, but the International Community had decided that he represented no strength in the political arena because he was near his term. To note that during the first years of his tenure and at the beginning of his second term, he was in good terms with the UN and the IDB from whom, according to the UN website, he received, among other aids, $4.2B to implement a mandatory and free education program for the children of Haiti; funds that were passed on to the administration of Mr. Michel Martelly.

Hypothesis 2: The presidential term limit obstructs the continued implementation of domestic policies.

Domestic policies are enacted and implemented with the hopes the International Community would fund them, which led to the country becoming and remaining dependent of foreign financial assistance. Popular beliefs have it that Presidents downright exhibit policy initiatives during their first term in order to gain popularity, laying then their nest for a second term. Popular beliefs also have it that Presidents, nearing their final term, are less likely to initiate new policies or take on new projects promoting government expansion because they have no electoral incentives to pursue. Domestic policies are considered as pertinent national and substantial legislative decision-making and problem solving measures taken by governments in order to promote democracy. (Kilpatrick, 2000). Chiozza and Goemans (2003) pondered that public policies are optimal and detailed strategies for the effective administration of government agencies. Whether just, equitable, and fair, they should survive even after their proponents are no longer in functions. They should be implemented by their successors regardless of political creed or political divergences (Zeigler, Pierskalla, and Mazumder, 2013). This is the principle of continuity that ensures that social programs continue to be executed even after their proponents are no longer presidents, allowing the people to continue to rip the seeds of these programs.

For Haiti, it is not necessarily so. Historically in Haiti, following the inauguration of new Presidents, good and democratic policies furthering the nations' economic well-being evaporate into oblivion to yield the place to new political agendas, thus putting the country in an incessant general policy renewal, not enchained to the harsh reality of the nation. Domestic policies include but are not limited to the identification of basic human rights such freedom of expression, right to education, right to healthcare, right to employment, etc., and the furthering of federal social programs with aims of fostering the durable and sustainable emancipation of the people.

The straightforward and overarching question "What are the impacts of the presidential term limits on domestic policies" has not failed to harvest adequate attention from the United Nations (UN) and the International Bank of Development (IBD), which had contributed tons of funds toward Haiti sustainable development. When referring to domestic policies, the UN and the IDB take into account fiscal policies and democratic policies for which Haitian leaders, according to various sources, are irresponsible (Armstrong, 2011).

Termed Presidents and Fiscal Policy

When Aristide was elected President of Haiti in 1991, he was very poor. Twenty years later, according to www.celebritynetworth.com, he is worth $800 million. He, René Préval and other interim Presidents such as Prosper Avril, Ertha Trouillot, Jean-Alexandre Boniface, among others are living in high luxury in Haiti while 99% of the population lives below the poverty line. Thus, Haitian leaders are seen as the most corrupted politicians in the world. They make their money by enacting bogus fiscal policies that attract the International Community, which is always keen to fund any federal program promoting social justice, sustainable development, or the welfare of the people. When these funds are disbursed, they keep them in their pockets or launch small projects that no way justify the amount of funds committed. Additionally, taxation brought a lot of money into the treasury. Conventional wisdom has it that taxes collected would have been invested back into the economy. The conditions of the country's national highways, the visible misery, the lack of care in hospitals, etc. is a living proof that the people do not benefit from fiscal policies.

At the end of their term, especially their second, Presidents are always eager to bring new fiscal policies either to collect taxes or to attract international assistance. It was in that line that the UN and the IBD did not hesitate to fund several of Préval's federal programs such the renovation of the International Airport, constructions of major highways, canalizations of several rivers, the mandatory and free education program, etc. Needless to say that much of these programs did not get to be started because Préval did not start them or these funds were utilized for other projects.

Hypothesis 3: Removing the presidential term limit might lead to necessary democracy in Haiti.

The concept "Democracy" deserves no introduction since it has been present in society since the beginning of times. However, to better illustrate its relationships to the phenomenon in question, we will explain its four components, which are government, active participation, protection of human rights, and social justice. The explanation of these key concepts will allow the researcher to uncover how they serve the basic needs of Haitian politics and economy (Moghadam, 2013). In a simpler term, democracy is defined as a political system where members participate in the decision-making process, where the government protects and guarantees human rights, and where all are provided equal opportunities for the pursuit of their happiness (Moghadam, 2013). The latter generates and drives the nation toward higher productivity and less dependence from their government.

Freedom of Expression

People participate in public affairs through elections where they elect and change governments at periodic intervals scheduled and set forth by the constitution. Should they like their Presidents, they would likely reelect them, should they not; these presidents would not be reelected. However, such a right to vote for whoever they want as many times they want is being trampled by the constitutional term limit. Voting or being involved in the decision-making process of their country is a basic individual right through which the people exercise their freedom of expression; a principle recognized by the Universal Declaration of Human Rights (1948). As such, it is guaranteed and must be protected by governments so to build a democratic environment. Hence, in Haiti, such a democratic right, is not being guaranteed nor is it being protected in the sense the term limit is not conducive to the will of the people for they are not allowed to elect their Presidents back to back, for more than two terms or indefinitely.

The referendum theory or simple a constitutional amendment may be applied in this case so to enable people to vote on whether Presidents should serve two consecutive terms. To respect this basic human right, the government must develop new strategies to amend Article 134.3 of the Constitution of 1987, which according to René Préval, as cited by Katz (2007) is at the root of the country's all sources of inconveniences.

Social Justice

As mentioned above, social justice drives the nation toward higher productivity and less dependence from their government. It is defined as the process of converting good intentions into viable actions or into actions that make positive differences in the lives of the people. It is the process of ensuring that all, especially the most disadvantaged communities, are getting a fair share of all available resources and equal access to opportunities and rights. It is also the act of the government to provide a fair system of law and due process while increasing individual incomes through the creation of jobs and the equal distribution of opportunities (Crethar and Ratts, n.d). The basic components of social justice are equity, access, harmony, and participation (Jost and Kay, 2010).

Because fair policies ceased to be implemented as soon as their proponents leave offices and because Presidents become corrupted at the end of their mandate, sitting governments fail to develop practical programs that will lead toward the emancipation and the self-sufficiency of the Haitian. Furthermore, term limit leads to disharmony in the sense several political groups claim to have the answers to the country's rising problems and thus organize countless of protestations against the government in place. Not a Haitian President can say that their tenure was free of protestations, civil unrests, crimes, kidnapping, coup d'état, threats of coup d'état, etc. If in other countries, especially in Western and European countries, the people voice their opinions through free elections, in Haiti, opinions are voiced through elections at first and then through protests as soon as presidents are perceived to go rogue. Very often, it will be the same people who elected him who will request that he leaves offices or else.

Literature Review

This section discusses "consecutive terms and interval period." Under the consecutive term concept, a term is worth five years and Presidents are only allowed to serve one term at a time, but no more than two. Under the interval period concept, which is a probation period that is usually five years, the clock resets and ex-Presidents are again eligible to run for the same office. A key aspect of the five-year probation period is that, since leaders are always attracted to power, throughout their first term they employ back door strategies through which they hand pick their successor while they remain powerful, influential, and instrumental in politics behind the scene (Vencovsky, 2009, p 15).

Presidential term limits publicizes successful and responsible transitions of leaderships. It is a political system's principle enabling the people to elect leaders through free and fair elections (Griner, 2009). For the past 25 years, the same political party, Famni Lavalas and other parties derived from [its] roots such as INITE and Repons Payzan have been democratically winning elections in Haiti where both Jean-Bertrand Aristide and René Préval had served two non-consecutive five-year terms each and Mr. Martely, actual President, is currently serving his first term. Many theorists believe that presidential term limit is a measure of performance and a best tool to hold leaders accountable as well as the most effective instrument for leaders to prove their worth to their both domestic and international audiences (Rhode and Simon, 1995). Like any other President from any other country, Haitian Presidents are also ranked based on how well their further diplomatic ties with foreign nations and how well their domestic policies promote necessary democracy (Tufte, (1975). Hence, it is to believe that presidents approaching the end of their term behave differently and are seen differently by the International Community, which may have strong impacts on the durable and suitable development of the country. Term limits may also have strong impacts on the democratic right of the people to continue to vote for whoever they want as many times they want.

A plethora of theories suggests that term limit is needed to promote diversity in governance and to increase maximum participation in elections while some argue that it is bad democracy in the sense it sustains a loss of political expertise and puts Presidents in complete political survival modes. Keele, Malhotra, and McCubbins (2009) contended that presidential term limits are intended to allow new classes of politicians to enter in functions at scheduled intervals and to this effect Vencovsky (2007) argued that presidential term limit is about democratic polity for it favors power alternations and enhances changes of political parties in governments. In other words, the constitutional term limit dismantles the old good boy network system by reducing the concentration of powers into the hands of the same web of traditional politicians. It promotes meritocracy and creates a mentality urging public service rather than political careers. It withstands deficiencies into social welfare and in the management of State assets, which could plunge the nation into unrecoverable chaos. As a legal limitation prescribed by popular constitutions of democratic nations, they also lead to a stopgap in commonsense policies.

According to Maeda and Nishikawa (2006), when Presidents are not allowed to run for another term, they will likely lean on to campaign for someone in their party. However, as Besley and Case, (1995) stated, the reelection of the same party depends on how well the outgoing President on how domestic policies lead to economic development and how well they enhance their relationships with Congress. Because of term limits, leaders remain democratically accountable because they perform more responsive to the demands of the people (Dettrey and Schwindt-Bayer (2009). Leaders, be they are democratic, autocratic, or dictatorial, even when in offices are always in constant campaign modes and thus are engaged in what de Mesquita et al. (2003) referred as political survival. They vehemently seek to maintain their positions, which allow them to continue to remain influential, having their hands on policies, dealing with domestic and international issues, etc. Unfortunately, democratic constitutions come to impose restrictions impeding individuals to remain in power for too long. Zeigler, Pierskalla, and Mazubmder (2013) defined it as "an observable and public known limitation on leader tenures." Haynes (2012) called it electoral punishments. According to Cheibub (2002), when nearing their terms, some Presidents lose their incentives to perform well, which in turn may affect the survival of their political party. According to McGlynn and Sylvester (2010), with term limits, new energy and news ideas are brought into governments.

Term limit is the weapon used by voters to get rid of leaders who are not working for the welfare of the people or politicians who place their personal ideologies above doing what is right (Nalder, 2007). It exists to prevent leaders from building their own political empire (Haynes, 2012). Chiozza and Goemans, (2011) and (McGlynn and Sylvester, 2010) argued that term limit impacts leaders' final stretch as public servants; they may lose the sense of urgency and motivation to engage in pushing commonsense policies, establishing politics of proximity to keep grass-roots movements energized, and even possibly, they may have the tendencies to delay elections so they can hold on to their positions a little longer. It is also shifts powers to special interests.

Who Can Be President of Haiti?

*A*ny *person who is a native-born Haitian, had never renounced his Haitian nationality, has attained to the age of 35 years, has resided in the country for five (5) consecutive years before the date of the elections, shall be eligible to the Office of the President of Haiti. Moreover, such a person shall have been relieved of his responsibilities if he has been handling public funds, he shall own at least one real property in Haiti, he shall have his habitual residence in the country, he shall enjoy civil and political rights, and he shall have never been sentenced to death, personal restraint or penal servitude or the loss of civil rights for a crime of ordinary law.*

Article 135, Chapter II1, Section A

The Constitution of Haiti of 1987 imposes several eligibility requirements on the Presidency: maturity, jus soli, jus sanguinis, ownership, fundamental rights, and good behaviors; all of these requirements must be met and fully satisfied at the time of taking office. As Gordon (1968) posit, "The Framers established eligibility qualifications in order to increase the chances of electing a person of patriotism, judgment, civic virtue, and with a sense of administration."

In addition, the Haitian Constitution shall have contended that these qualifications apply solely to first-termed Presidents because, according to article 134.4, shall sitting presidents desire to run for a second term, they shall meet another requirement; they shall satisfy a five-year probation because two consecutive terms are, in no case, allowed by the

Constitution. Shall they meet the probation period, run and win to serve a second term; they are again compelled to satisfy another requirement; they are not permitted to run for a third term. Hereafter, do they lose their civil and political rights to ever be eligible to run for Presidents again?

Does such a constitutional restriction [probation period and no third term] do justice to current and past Presidents? Are not they having their rights trampled by the proponents of such a disposition? Why do Presidents have to serve cumulatively instead of consecutively? Was this article well socialized when the people voted that Constitution? Is presidential term limits bad or necessary democracy? Is not it because of presidential term limits that rogue politicians routinely lead the people into protesting against Presidents they, themselves, vote or is not it because of presidential term limits that Presidents, knowing they will not face their constituents for a third time, become corrupted and dishonest; thus facing coup d'états, threats of coup d'états, uprising, pressures from the opposition to leave powers, demonstrations, civil wars, insecurity, etc.?

The next chapter of this study will provide answers to all of these probing and thought-provoking questions.

History of Haiti's Presidential Term Limits

After the fall of the Duvaliers who had governed Haiti for about 30 years, a new class of politicians abruptly rose with the mission to re-orientate the political destiny of the impoverished nation. Their first acts were to enact policies on who were eligible to participate in Haitian politics and to statute on the maximum term limits on leadership tenures as a means to prevent the same person to remain in offices for too long. Since the enactment of the Haitian constitution of 1987, Haitians have democratically elected Presidents such as Jean-Bertrand Aristide, René Préval, and currently Michel Martelly.

Such a constitutional restriction forces Presidents out of their offices as soon as they begin to acquire political maturity and administrative wisdom to master their social bonds with the people. It influences continuity in public administration where presidents have never gotten to be comfortable to fully apply and execute sound policies. As noted above, Jean-Bertrand Aristide and René Préval, as members of the leading political party, Fanmi Lavalas, served two non-consecutive mandates respectively, which is to show that the people are likely to reelect someone as many times they want or as many times the Constitution allows it. Préval did not seek a third term because the constitution in place, under no circumstance, allows a third term. Aristide could not because, halfway to his second term, the United States of America set foot in Haiti to remove him from offices and thereafter to send him into exile in South-Africa where he remained from 2004 to 2011.

As it is the case for other democratic nations, while Presidents are not allowed to run for two consecutive terms or other terms, article 134.3 does not prevent the same political parties to continue to participate in elections. It was to that end that Fanmi Lavalas was able to govern the country for about 20 years with Jean-Bertrand Aristide and René Préval elected twice by the people. Was not for a technicality into the electoral law that excluded Fanmi Lavalas from the electoral contests of 2011, still today, Fanmi Lavalas would have continued to win presidential elections because Fanmi Lavalas is dubbed as the Left Wing of Haiti's politics, and as such, is working toward economic and political freedoms. Michel Martelly, who had won in 2011 under Repons Payizan, a party formed of old members of Famni Lavalas, will pass the torch to someone else in 2016. More likely, he will mentor someone in his party, Mouvman Tèt Kale (MTK) or a close friend to replace him while he will be campaigning during his probation period in order to run again in 2021.

Katz (2007) pondered that ex-President René Préval was the first Haitian to publically point out the limitation to serve two consecutive terms as "the single greatest threat to Haiti's long-term stability." According to Préval, cited by the author, a change in Article 134.3 of the Constitution would bring political stability in Haiti where insecurity, corruption, and misery had been plaguing the nation since the Day of its Independence.

Presidential term limits capture time elected leaders remain in offices and the paramount role of elections, which build political parties and political leaders' reputation and their incentives to serve the public. Haiti is at an intersection where the people are requiring more and more from their government. Now, more than ever, the people are using popular social networks to voice their opinions on how and by whom they rather be governed. The government of Martelly is being referred as [predatorial] as well as favoring a minority of light-skinned Haitians over the majority of Black Haitians. Currently, there are various protestations suggesting the return of Fanmi Lavalas to powers because, according to Dr. Maryse Narcisse, the party's Number 2, Jean-Bertrand Aristide has been the only President [even throughout both his exile in America and South Africa respectively] who has been placing the welfare of the people before his own (Haiti Observer, 2013).

As stated above, there are not too much researches questioning whether the presidential term limit is bad or necessary democracy for Haiti. Such a study is worth pursuing because it will allow the researcher to provide argumentative tools to students in Law, Political Science and Diplomacy fields. It will also allow politicians and humanitarian organizations to understand new roots of Haiti's political and economic stability. Moreover, it has the potential to spark debates on whether to remove the mandate, extend it to a third term, or whether to treat such a limitation as a violation of the democratic right of the people. A study on Haiti's presidential term limits is important for both the elected and the governed and as Katz (2007) stated it is an essential component to build democracy and to allow the most effective Haitian political leader to remain in functions so to continue to effectively serve his or her constituents.

Methodology

This paper is qualitative in nature for it aims to explore Haiti's presidential term limit in order to promote understanding and awareness on how it impacts political stability and how it violates the democratic right of the people. The researcher will seek knowledge toward establishing relationships and toward defining key concepts, collect, generalize, interpret, and analyze the data (Denzin, 1970).

The research will utilize the case study and the grounded theory approaches. The former approach is an empirical inquiry that investigates a phenomenon where answers to support a claim are placed into perspectives (Yin, 1984). In this instance, case studies will be Haiti's tumultuous political history spread out over a period of 25 years where the same political parties have been governing Haiti. The case studies will range from the tenure of Jean-Bertrand Aristide to Michel Martelly passing through René Préval except that René Préval and Martelly had won the elections respectively under INITE and Repons Payizan; two parties formed of partisans and old members of Fanmi Lavalas because Lavalas could not participate in the last elections based on the principle that only the President of the party can register such a party in elections. Aristide was out of the country and he did not want to relinquish his powers to any of his comrades. Note that Mr. Martelly is going rogue by publically demonstrating that he has no ties whatsoever to Lavalas and that Haiti is under and will remain under a new leadership for at least 20 years.

Glaser and Strauss (1967) posited that grounded theory enables researchers to uncover or generate theories from data that are systematically obtained. Dey (1999) stated that the grounded theory is done through analytical procedures and sampling strategies. It uses several data collections such as in-depth interviews, observations, focus groups, etc. in order to collect sensitive data. The other types of qualitative approaches will not provide the latitude to conduct a joint analysis of data collected nor they are framed as to allow researchers to follow and set guidelines for the interviews and to identify the process of interview coding through which recurring themes and subthemes can be found.

Framework of the Study

This study will use a conceptual framework to help the researcher identifies the problem, find suitable literatures, and clarifies and formulates overreaching research questions, goals, and objectives (Barbour, 1999). Creswell (2013) stated the main feature of the conceptual framework is that it lays down the blueprint for the research. Carol et al. (2007) defined conceptual framework as a set of theoretical assumptions, principles, and rules working together to glue the research.

The researcher will formulate various assumptions of the impacts of Haiti's presidential term limits on diplomacy, domestic policies, and democracy. He will refer to the extensive literature review to pluck out theories and principles ensuring they are meshed together in order to provide maps that build coherence to the investigation and that explain propositions or hypotheses. Moreover, the conceptual framework will drive the methodology while explaining key constructs and terms.

Such a framework applies to the phenomenon in question based on the fact that little is known on the topic and it enables the researcher to connect all the aspects of Haitian's socio and geo- economics and geo-politics to better position the phenomenon along with its identified problem, purpose, etc. within found theories and methodologies (Creswell, 2013).

Respondents

The methodology will consist of two sets of interviews; one tailored for representatives of the government as well as high ranking members of political parties who will be asked overarching questions in order to allow them to share their knowledge of the presidential limit, provide their thoughts on how it impacts the activities aforementioned. The target audience will consist of 30 participants. The second set of interviews will be targeted toward officials of local governance such as Mayors, ASECs, and CASECs. We select them because they directly represent the people in their respective commune. They will be asked whether they think the people should be the ones to decide how many terms Presidents can serve. Based on their answers, the referendum theory will be discovered. 291 people will be randomly chosen as participants for this second set of structured interviews.

Sampling

Hague et al. (2011) posited that sampling is the process of obtaining information about an entire population by examining only a portion of it. Our sampling strategy will revolve around identifying political cases with relevant characteristics that will provide enough data for the researcher to support that term limit does indeed impact foreign relations and domestic policies. First, we will collect 25 years of political history, analyze them as case studies and prove that for the past quarter of century, the same party has been winning elections and that the five-year interval creates a stopgap in both foreign and domestic policies. Second, pertinent data will be collected from interviews. The researcher will use Emails, video-teleconferences and phone calls to contact the first target audience and surface-mail to contact the second segment.

Data Collection and Data Analysis

This section presents the analysis and the interpretation of data, which was collected through two sets of interviews; the first one is structural in nature where 291 participants were asked to answer whether they subjective thoughts on the topic on hand. Because the interview was structured; the 10 questions were closed-ended to state answers like Agree, Disagree, Not Sure, and I Don't Know. Using the Medoid Clustering, after compilation, data was scientifically processed using NVivo to sort the questions by their answers and to determine whether the results match the observations of the research, which is that Haiti's presidential term limits do indeed impact the long term stability of the country. The interview captures participants' familiarity with the concepts of term limits, participative democracy, government corruption public and foreign policies, and social justice. The objectives have been achieved and the results presented in this chapter demonstrate the potential and the need to remove the five-year probation or to grant the people the legal authority to decide how whether presidents should serve indefinitely.

Limitations

The first limitation of the study was the fact that there are no previous researches about the phenomenon to study. The researcher will be forced to rely on the locals' knowledge of the situation as well their thoughts. In light of that, reliability and authenticity of data collected will be at stake and might affect findings and the conclusion of the research. To ensure reliability and authenticity, participants will be chosen randomly and will not interact with each other. Regarding biases, the researcher has no political preference or affiliation. He will try to remain as neutral as possible to reduce subjectivity and address weaknesses throughout data analysis.

Ethical Considerations

Ethical concerns include various aspects such as privacy of sample collected, participant's political affiliations, etc. Participants will be briefed on the purpose of the research and how their participation might be bringing positive changes onto the political construct of Haiti (Lewis, 2007). Participants will fill the consent form in accordance with the guidelines and purpose of the research study (Lewis, 2007).

The present chapter is dedicated to the presentation of results of the survey conducted with members of the local govern-ance and that of the civil society. The researcher presents the socio-demographic characteristics of the respondents along with their significance for the research question of interest.

Socio-Demographic Variables of Sample

The total number of local residents, members of the civil society, who participated in the present survey constituted 291 persons, and the sample was current and ex government officials and students. They were divided into males and females and their socio-demographic data and results of socio-demographic analysis are shown in Figure 1.

Figure 1   Gender of Respondents

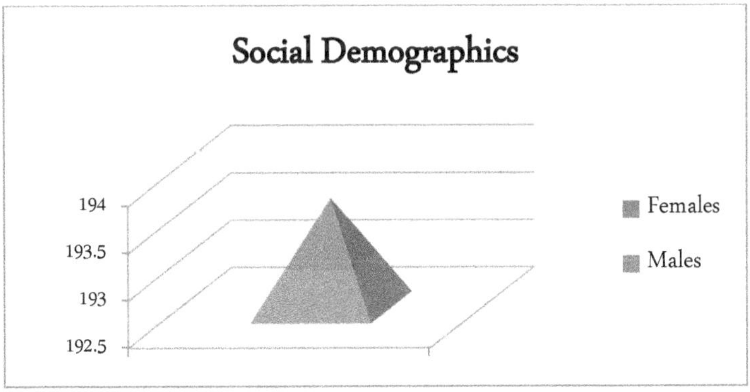

As one can see from Figure 1, the portion of male respondents was significantly higher (193, which is 66.32%) than that of females (98, which is 33.67%). The age of respondents varied from 23 to 50 years old, with the most populous category being those aged 26-36. The next portion of socio-demographic data elicited from respondents pertained directly to Haiti's presidential term limits. The statistics on their answers can be seen in Figure 2.

Figure 2   Data Regarding Presidential Term Limits

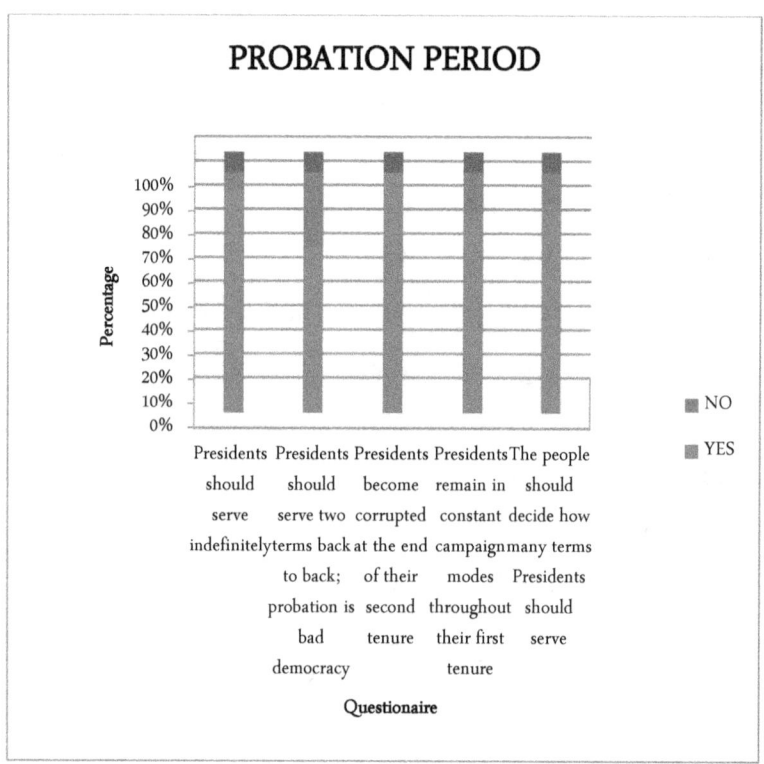

As evidence in Figure 2 suggests, this section of the survey collects data about Haiti's presidential and their impacts on the country's stability. Respondents were provided a 5 question questionnaire where they were to answer yes or no. 92.50% (268) believe presidents should be permitted to serve indefinitely while 0.07% (23) stated otherwise. It was also found that the probation should be removed because it is bad democracy for the country. 69.07% (201) respondents contend that, not allowing Presidents to serve back to back, the probation period forces

Presidents to remain in constant campaign modes throughout their first tenure (83.16% ; 242). It is also found that decision (86.25% ; 245) for a President to serve two consecutive terms or to serve a third, a fourth, or indefinitely should be left to the people themselves instead of bunch of legislators who are constantly out of touch.

Figure 2   Data Impacts of the Presidential Term Limits

Respondents were asked to choose among a pool of suggested benefits and to rank them by order of significance from 1 to 5, with 1 being the lowest level of importance and effectiveness, and 5 being the highest level. Rating from 1 to 5 indicated the intensity of influence of each factor. The table shows that to a larger or lesser extent, all named factors were considered as highly influential on the participant's pool of answers.

Figure 3   Impacts of the Probation Period

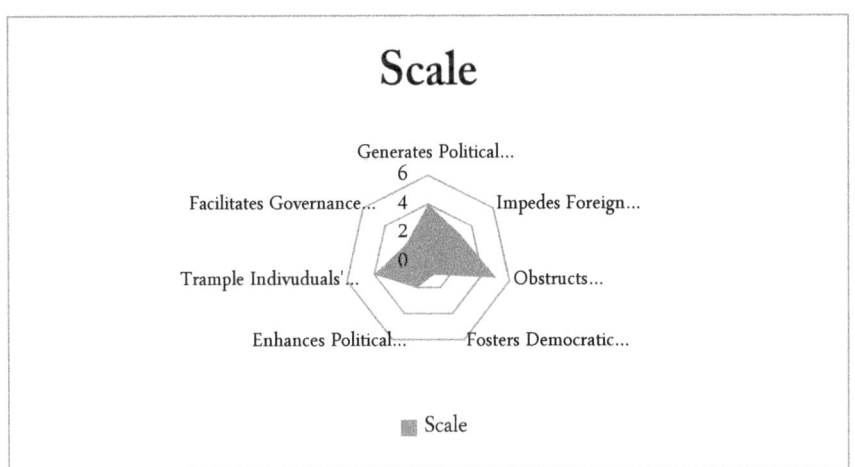

Data collected from figure 3 had shown that the people of Haiti argued that presidential term limits, especially the five-year probation period, does not facilitate governance diversity in the sense that the possibilities for another political to win elections is not likely and in the sense, if history teaches them anything, is that political parties remain in powers for at least 20 years. That happened with Lavalas and the same thing is on the verge to be happening with Mouvman Tèt Kale.

The respondents also state that the probation period tramples individuals' freedoms for the people should have been allowed to vote for Presidents back to back or as many times they wish. It prevents leaders from acquiring political maturity and obstructs the implementation of public policies, placing the country in constant changes in leaderships as well as it impedes foreign relations where the International Community has been reluctant to negotiate with outgoing Presidents who may become corrupted when approaching the end of their mandate.

Summary

At the aftermath of the earthquake of 12 January 2010, the world has been demonstrating hard interests in the development of Haiti. International aids were dispatched and huge funds were committed toward the reconstruction of the country. Lots of diplomatic ties and the need to improve the government were being developed so to create an environment where foreign assistance could be flown transparently. Thus, this study holds an important stand in the present scenario because diplomacy and democracy are gaining strides and it is becoming important that the UN and its allies negotiate with full termed Presidents and that outgoing Presidents do not implement fiscal policies just to fill their pockets with taxes collected and money given to better the lives of the people. This study is also conducted as a recommendation to place the right to elect into the hands of the people themselves.

The study have been conducted to investigate the impact of presidential term limits on democracy and social justice and various supporting material has been provided for clarification of research topic and also, the research methodology and data collection analysis section have been briefed for the introduction of way of conducting the research study. The Constitution of Haiti of 1987 imposed the five-year interval as a means to promote political diversity and to allow other candidates to come play their partition in the political field. It also encourages Presidents to perform well through the establishment of social justice policies whether or not they are seeking reelections. To this end, while waiting to become re-eligible, they are compelled to remain active through the implementation of politics of proximity, which enable them to stay close and to listen to their constituents.

On the other hand, throughout their first tenure, Presidents are bound to perform well in the preparation of their next tenure. As such, they operate in unceasing campaign modes, taking advantage of every opportunity to pose for photos with the most vulnerable communities and to broadcast news story placing them in the spectrum of the machine of progress. Furthermore, should they have enacted popular policies, after their first term, depending on who replace them; the implementation of their policies may be discontinued because the new President may come with new policies and new staff members, which affect the continuity of welfare policies and that of governmental institutions.

To remediate to this situation, it is proven necessary to call for an amendment of the Constitution so to apply therein the rule of majority through which the people will vote to either keep or remove the probationary period or extend or remove the ten-year requirement to hold the country's highest office.

Conclusion

The bottom line up front is that in Haiti, Presidents are not permitted to run for reelections indefinitely whereas there is no limit restriction for CASECs, ASECs, Mayors, Deputies, and Senators. The rationale behind Haiti's presidential term limit is that it prevents powers from being concentrated into the hands of a clan of politicians for more than 10 years. Griner (2009) stated that term limits enforces democracy and it ensures long-term stability and diversity in political governance through which scheduled transitions leading to new political establishments taking places. Vencovsky (2007, p.19) called it the best manifestation of democracy for it allows politicians to compete for powers as well as it promotes participative democracy through which the people are guaranteed the rights to choose their leaders and hold them accountable for their policies both foreign and domestic. On the other hand, if governments are by the people and for the people; why does the form of government have to be derived from the constitution? Other trend suggests that term limit is a downright violation of the people democratic right to vote indefinitely for the leaders they want (de Mesquita et al., 2003).

We have compared several perspectives of the phenomenon, observed 30 years of Haiti's political history and the current political tenure, and conducted two set interviews whose participants were randomly chosen; we uncovered that presidential term limit is the most complex in Haiti and it negatively impacts foreign relations, domestic policies, and democracy. We advocated for the amendment of Article 134, Section of the Constitution of Haiti of 1987 so to remove the five-year interval, allowing Presidents to serve an additional third term or to leave the decision whether Presidents may serve a third, fourth, or a fifth to the people themselves.

References

Archibold, R., C. (2011). Popular Carnival Singer Is Elected President of Haiti in a Landslide. Retrieved from http://www.nytimes.com/2011/04/05/world/americas/05haiti.html?_r=0

Armstrong, B. (2011). Ne touche pas ma constitution: Pressures and presidential term limits. Department of Political Science. Northwestern University.

Moghadam, V., M. (2013). What is democracy? Promises and perils of the Arab Spring. Current Sociology July 2013 61: 393-408

Barbour, R. S. (1999). The case for combining qualitative and quantitative approaches in health services research. Journal of Health Services Research Policy, 4, 39– 43

Besley T., & Case, A. (1995). Does electoral accountability affect economic policy choices? Evidence from gubernatorial term limits." Quarterly Journal of Economics 110 (3): 769–98

Carol et al. (2007). A conceptual framework for implementation fidelity. Retrieved from http://www.implementationscience.com/content/2/1/40

Chiebub, J., A. (2002). Minority governments, Deadlock Situations, and the survival of presidential democracies. Comparative Political Studies, April 2002; vol. 35, 3: pp. 284-312

Chiozza G. & Goemans H. E.(2003). Peace through insecurity. Journal of Conflict Resolution 47 (4): 443

Chiozza G. & Goemans H. E. (2011). Leaders and international conflict. New York: Cambridge University Press

Crethar, H., C. & Ratts, M., J. (n.d). Why social justice is a counseling concern. Retrieved from http://www.txca.org/images/tca/Template/TXCSJ/Why_social_justice _is_a_counseling_concern.pdf

Creswell, J. (2013). Qualitative inquiry & research design: Choosing among five approaches. Thousand Oaks, CA: Sage Publications, Inc.

de Mesquita et al. (2003). The logic of political survival. Cambridge, MA: MIT Press Constitution of the Republic of Haiti (1987). Retrieved from http://pdba.georgetown.edu/constitutions/haiti/haiti1987.html

Denzin,K., N. (1970). The research act. Chicago: Aldine Publishing.

Dettrey, B., J. & Schwindt-Bayer, L., A. (2009). Voter turnout in presidential democracies. Comparative Political Studies, October 2009; vol. 42, 10: pp. 1317-1338.

Dey, I. (1999). Grounding grounded theory guidelines for qualitative inquiry. San Diego. Academic Press. http://en.wikipedia.org/wiki/Social_democracy - cite_ref-149

Eatwell, R. (2011). Contemporary political ideologies. Continuum International Publishing Group, 2011. p. 91.

Forman, M., J., Lang, H., & Chandler. A. (2011). The role of the Haitian diaspora in building Haiti back better. Retrieved from http://csis.org/publication/role-haitian-diaspora-building-haiti-back-better

Glaser, B., G. (1967). The discovery of grounded theory: Strategies for qualitative research. New York: Aldine de Gruyter

Goldberg, M., L. (2013). Haiti three years on: facts and figures from the earthquake recovery. Retrieved from http://www.undispatch.com/haiti-three-years-on-facts-and-figures-from-the-earthquake-recovery

Gordon, C. (1968). Who can be President of the United States: The Unresolved Enigma, 28 Md. L. Rev. 1.

Griner, S. (2009). Term limits can check corruption and promote political accountability. Retrieved from http://www.americasquarterly.org/pros-and-cons-of-term-limits

Hague, M. et al. (2011). Sampling methods in social research. Retrieved from http://www.google.com/search?sourceid=navclient&ie=UTF8&rlz=1T4GZGN_enDE488DE488&q=what+is+sampling+research#

Haiti Observer (2013). Dr. Maryse Narcisse called manman Lavalas by the crowd. Retrieved from http://www.haitiobserver.com/blog/dr-maryse-narcisse-called-manman-lavalas-by-the-crowd.html

Hanson, S. (2006). In Haiti, stability remains elusive. Retrieved from http://www.cfr.org/haiti/haiti-stability-remains-elusive/p11392

Harrington, M. (2011), Socialism: past and future. Reprint edition of original published in 1989. New York, New York, USA: Arcade Publishing, 2011. p. 56.

Haynes K. (2012). Lame ducks and coercive diplomacy: Do executive term limits reduce the effectiveness of democratic threats?" Journal of Conflict Resolution 56 (5): 771–98.

Jost, J., T. & Kay, A., C. (2010). Social justice: History, theory, and research. Retrieved from http://www.psych.nyu.edu/jost/Social%20Justice_%20History,%20The ory,%20&%20Research.pdf

Katz, J., M. (2007). Haiti's Préval seeks to amend term limit. Retrieved fromhttp://www.foxnews.com/printer_friendly_wires/2007Oct17/0,46 7HaitiPresident,00.html

Keele, L., Malhotra, N., & McCubbins, H., C. (2009). Do term limits restrain State fiscal policy? Approaches for causal Inference in assessing the effects of legislative institutions. Retrieved from http://www.personal.psu.edu/ljk20/termlimits.pdf

Kilpatrick, D., G. (2000). Definition of public policies and law. Retrieved from http://www.musc.edu/vawprevention/policy/definition.shtml

Lewis, J., E. (2007). German exile politics: the social democratic executive committee in the Nazi era. University of California Press, 2007. p. 215.

Maeda, K. & Nishikawa, M. (2006). Duration of party control in parliamentary and presidential governments: A study of 65 democracies, 1950 to 1998. Comparative Political Studies, vol. 39, 3: pp. 352-374

Mark T., B. (2004), The battle for Asia: From decolonization to globalization. Oxon, England, UK; New York, New York, USA: Routledge Curzon, 2004. p. 73.

McGlynn, A., J. & Sylvester, D., E. (2010). Assessing the effects of municipal term limits on fiscal policy in U.S. cities. State and local government Review 42(2) 118-132

Nalder, K. (2007). The effect of state legislative term limits on voter turnout. State Politics & Policy Quarterly, June 20, 2007; vol. 7, 2: pp. 187-210

Rhode D., W. & Simon D., M. (1985). "Presidential vetoes and congressional response: A study of institutional conflict." American Journal of Political Science 29 (3): 397–427

The Universal Declaration of Human Rights . (1948). Retrieved from http://www.un.org/en/documents/udhr/

Tufte E. R. (1975). Determinants of the outcomes of midterm congressional elections. American Political Science Review 69 (3): 812–26 http://en.wikipedia.org/wiki/Social_democracy - cite_ref-9

Upchurch, M., Graham, J., T. &, Mathers, A. (2009). The crisis of social democratic trade unionism in Western Europe: the search for alternatives. Surrey, England, UK; Burlington, Vermont, USA: Ashgate Publishing, 2009. p. 51

Vencovsky, D. (2007). Presidential term limits in Africa. Conflict Trends, Issue 2 (2007)

Voices of America (2012). Concern for stability in Haiti. Retrieved from http://editorials.voa.gov/content/concern-for-stability-in-haiti 141513303/1493304.html

Yin, R. K. (1984). Case study research: Design and methods. Newbury Park, CA: Sage.

Zeigler, S., Pierskalla, J., H. & Mazumder, S. (2013). War and the reelection motive: Examining the effect of term limits. Journal of Conflict Resolution March 13, 2013

About the Author

Bobb doctors in Law and Public Policy at Walden University, he received three Master degrees from Webster University, and he also earned in Bachelor Degree in Law from the University of Haiti. He is a regular contributor to 5 Magazine where he publishes articles dealing with ongoing issues of his native country Haiti.

After publishing several novels and poetry books, Bobb decided it was time for different challenges, explorations, and experiments. He wanted to apply his knowledge toward contributing to greater good and henceforward he began conducting researches on Haiti's permanent root of crisis such as Brain Drain, Social Justice, Food Insecurity, Decentralization, and Immigration among others.

"I want to tap into the Haitian human capital; that target of the population that writers and the media tend to neglect," he wrote in one of his articles. Consequently, Bobb writes no longer to entertain, but to encourage Haitians to think strategically and critically and "hopefully they will take actions toward their self-actualization and toward the sustainable development of their respective community."

The various researches conducted and published by Bobb have a recurring theme "empowerment and self-empowerment" which can be done through education and individual emancipation.

"I don't write for fame; I write hoping that my message will land into the hands of the right audience; that audience deciding for the country and that audience that keeps asking to whomever are listening

"What the country can do for me" instead of "what I can do for my country."

"The people of Haiti are my primary valid and reliable sources of researches; I talk to them, they tell me what they think, and I put them on paper. And the credits go them for I simply broadcast their sufferings and their desires for hopes and opportunities," he claimed during an interview with Alex St-Surin.

Bobb can be contacted at bobjrusso@yahoo.com.

www.ingramcontent.com/pod-product-compliance
Lightning Source LLC
Chambersburg PA
CBHW070322290526
45791CB00003B/1213

9 781497 327276